Teaching Writing Through Poetry

Teaching Writing

About the Series

This series for K-12 and collegiate writing and English teachers, educators, curriculum specialists, and preservice teacher education candidates provides methods, pedagogy and practical exercises in the teaching of writing.

Books in the series explore the vast array of ideas, strategies and topics that actively engage students in developing skills that will help them become better writers, critical readers and critical thinkers. These fresh methodologies will expand students' ideas on what writing means, as well as what learning can mean. Various approaches in the series will rejuvenate instructors and feed educators' own desires as lifelong learners.

Each book is meant to make the educators lives both easier and more fulfilling, as the texts in this series include a plethora of writing exercises, prompts and approaches. Many titles will benefit educators from various disciplines who are interested in implementing more writing into their curriculum. Feel free to reach out with questions, ideas, or anything else: kvm@drexel.edu

Titles in Series:

Teaching Writing Through Journaling by Kathleen Volk-Miller
Teaching Writing Through Poetry by Jason Schneiderman

Teaching Writing Through Poetry

Understanding Poetic Form and
Its Power to Unleash Creative Expression

Jason Schneiderman

BLOOMSBURY ACADEMIC
NEW YORK • LONDON • OXFORD • NEW DELHI • SYDNEY

BLOOMSBURY ACADEMIC

Bloomsbury Publishing Inc, 1359 Broadway, New York, NY 10018, USA
Bloomsbury Publishing Plc, 50 Bedford Square, London, WC1B 3DP, UK
Bloomsbury Publishing Ireland, 29 Earlsfort Terrace, Dublin 2, D02 AY28, Ireland

BLOOMSBURY, BLOOMSBURY ACADEMIC and the Diana logo are trademarks of Bloomsbury Publishing Plc

First published in the United States of America 2026

Copyright © Bloomsbury Publishing Inc, 2026

Cover image: © istock/Oleksandr Blishch

All rights reserved. No part of this publication may be: i) reproduced or transmitted in any form, electronic or mechanical, including photocopying, recording or by means of any information storage or retrieval system without prior permission in writing from the publishers; or ii) used or reproduced in any way for the training, development or operation of artificial intelligence (AI) technologies, including generative AI technologies. The rights holders expressly reserve this publication from the text and data mining exception as per Article 4(3) of the Digital Single Market Directive (EU) 2019/790.

Bloomsbury Publishing Inc does not have any control over, or responsibility for, any third-party websites referred to or in this book. All internet addresses given in this book were correct at the time of going to press. The author and publisher regret any inconvenience caused if addresses have changed or sites have ceased to exist, but can accept no responsibility for any such changes.

A catalog record for this book is available from the Library of Congress

ISBN: HB: 978-1-4758-7477-8
PB: 978-1-4758-7478-5
ePDF: 979-8-7651-6053-4
eBook: 978-1-4758-7479-2

Typeset by Deanta Global Publishing Services, Chennai, India
Printed and bound in the United States of America

For product safety related questions contact productsafety@bloomsbury.com.

To find out more about our authors and books visit www.bloomsbury.com and sign up for our newsletters.

Contents

Introduction: Form Is Content 1

1 An Arbitrary Order Still Makes Demands: The Abecedarian 7

2 Looking in the Broken Mirror: The Ghazal 17

3 The Divided Self Is a Field of Play: The Sonnet 25

4 Satellites and Snowballs: Writing the Villanelle 41

5 An Obsession Is a Tether: The Sestina 49

6 One Step Forward, Two Steps Back: The Pantoum 59

7 Write What You See: The Ekphrastic Poem 65

8 Structuring Devices: Rhythm, Rhyme, and Line 73

Bibliography 87
About the Author 89

Introduction
Form Is Content

There are a lot of books to teach you about writing. And there are a lot of books to teach you about poetry. And there are a lot of books to teach you about poetic form. So why use this one? Why listen to me?

Because I take the position that form *is* content. Each poetic structure demands a particular kind of thinking. If you write a villanelle, you have to be obsessed. You can't repeat two lines over and over again without having some sort of *idée fixe*. You can't write a sonnet without engaging some kind of internal division. You can't write a ghazal without approaching a single concern from multiple angles. Poetic form doesn't just require a set of repetitions and patterns: it requires a particular rhetorical approach. Each poetic form is a particular kind of thinking.

Many people—at least to my mind—make two mistakes when they think about poetic form. The first is that they think that poetry is just a shapeless flow of feelings onto the page. For these writers and readers, poems *have no rules*. Poetry is freedom, but poetry also cannot be judged or evaluated or improved or shaped. The *only* concern is the feelings that produced it. The second mistake is treating poetic form as a sort of incidental container. For this group, poetic form feels like a Jell-O mold—you can pour in any Jell-O, and the Jell-O is the same, regardless of whether it's shaped like a castle or a dome or a cube or a star. I think that all poetry is formal—that all poetry is asking you to pay attention to its structuring devices: lineation, repetition, rhythm, sound. But feelings are not the easy part—evoking an emotional experience in the reader is actually a fairly complex and difficult task that poetry is particularly adept at. Poetry actually has lots of rules—even if it has few referees—because it's so hard to make someone else feel what we are feeling. And in following my instructions, you'll end up having to follow them.

I also believe that any time you tell an artist a rule, there is a special little part of their brain that comes to life wondering how they can break that rule. And much great art comes from breaking the rules. But any broken rule in one generation can quickly become a new rule for the next generation.

In this book, I will guide you through how to treat each poetic form as a structure with meaning. I often say to my more advanced students that the poetic line must be shaped to the phrasing and the phrasing must be shaped to the line. Poetic form is a bit like curfew—it sets limits on your freedom, but it also makes asserting your freedom that much more exciting.

Poetry is also surprisingly social. Molly Peacock describes falling in love with poetry this way: "I was connected not only to poems, but to other people who have read them" (2). Many famous poems have been written as challenge poems—when two poets give themselves the same assignment and see who can write the better poem. You can also play the game cooperatively (rather than competitively) and see how different poets respond to the same demands. One way to think about this book is as a set of challenges for you and your classmates or friends. Sharing poems can be intimidating, but when everyone in the group is sharing poems that had the same demands, it can be a great way to build community. If you are a business major, think of it as a team-building exercise. If you are a lone wolf, think of it as setting yourself apart from the pack. Every single time a poet writes a new poem, it expands what's possible for everyone who reads that poem.

I will also ask you to write a lot of poems that you would probably not write on your own. As I often say to my students, when they complain that my assignments ask them to do things that they wouldn't do on their own, I respond *that's what school is*. I usually follow up by reminding them that I don't *stop* them from writing on their own. But more importantly, the value of an education is being asked to learn skills and study facts that you wouldn't encounter on your own. My college students often think of general education (where you have to take a history requirement, and a social studies requirement, and creative expression requirement, and so on) as a chore—a set of hoops to be jumped through in order to get the degree. As the Indigo Girls sang, "I spent four years prostrate to the higher mind/ got my paper and I was free." But those hoops are there to make sure that anyone with a college education has been exposed to a wide variety of bodies of knowledge, analytical lenses, and problem-solving techniques. I think about poetic form in the same way. Knowing the ghazal, and the sestina, and the sonnet doesn't mean that those are the only kinds of poems you'll write, and in fact, it may inform your poetic practice in a way that no reader would ever be able to see the influence of those structures on your later work.

The internet has made learning about poetic structure easier than ever—but it's also put a lot of partial, erroneous, and flawed information out there. I was once contacted by a colleague to let me know that a student had written about one of my poems, but when he sent me his student's essay, I could see he had used a bootlegged version of my poem that had structural errors. Should I be grateful that the student liked my work? Should I be angry that my poems are circulating in incorrect forms? Probably both. But to aid you in your searches, I will direct you toward two reliable and authoritative online archives that have a wealth of poems and information about poems: The Poetry Foundation (poetryfoundation.org) and the American Academy of Poets (poets.org). In some ways, these two internet assemblages have replaced anthologies in a lot of classrooms. For this collection, I have either used work in the public domain or I have written the poems myself. In writing the formal poems myself, I am paying tribute to John Hollander's *Rhyme's Reason*, which is a far more comprehensive collection of poetic form. Hollander wrote each formal poem about writing the form it is written in. It's quite an achievement, and I highly recommend his collection.

You may be tempted to skip the writing process altogether and just ask ChatGPT to do the assignments for you. Many of my students are so afraid of "doing it wrong" that they just ask for the work to be done by robots who live inside the internet. But the thing about artificial intelligence is that while it *is* artificial, it's *not* intelligent. All that large language models can do is predict what word would be most likely to come next *if* a person were writing. And those predictions are now sufficiently accurate that ChatGPT probably can write you a fairly good villanelle or abecedarian or ghazal, but you'll be missing out on a crucial part of the experience. Writing is a thinking process. In writing things down, you make discoveries. Part of the power of doing an exercise is what you learn from the process. And in sharing your work, you'll learn from each other's processes. If you outsource that to a computer, you're giving up the chance to fully experience what it means to be human. The truth is that you get good at what you do. If you keep writing poems, you'll get good at writing poems. If you lie about doing your assignments because they were done by an artificial intelligence, you'll get good at lying. Lying is a useful skill, but I'd rather be able to write a villanelle.

Many of these chapters began as essays in a column called "The Literary Anatomy" that was published in the magazine *Teachers and Writers*. A few passages are adapted from online courses that I have taught to introductory students. For the most part, I have extensively rewritten them because they were written solely with teachers as the audience, while this book is meant to welcome students and teachers alike. The essay on the line is the closest to the one that was originally published.

Whether you are reading this on a screen or a page, I'd encourage you to write by hand; to have a notebook and a pen you like, to make the act of writing physical and material; analog rather than digital. The first reason is that it's less distracting. Pieces of paper never get push notifications or phone calls. Pieces of paper don't underline the words you misspelled and demand that you fix them before you write the next word. The second reason is that your drafts persist. If you're typing away and you erase a paragraph or a stanza or a title, it's simply gone. Pages and ink keep your words there, even after you've crossed them out. If you write ten pages and keep two, you still have the eight pages as a testament to what you did for the past day or so. The third reason is that it forces you to work in drafts. When you go to type a final draft of your manuscript pages, you will find yourself making different choices as you look at what you've written.

One last note. If you pick up most books of poetry, or most poetry journals, you'll notice that free verse is the dominant mode of contemporary US poetry. So why bother learning all about poetic form if that is not what is mostly getting published? Good question. Glad you asked. The first is that free verse requires a well-tuned ear, and that working in form can teach you to pay attention to line breaks, rhythms, and structures in a way that will make you a better poet in free verse. It's a bit like how musicians play scales in order to be better at playing symphonies. The second reason is that most poets do know poetic form and recognize a villanelle or sestina or ghazal when they see it. If you want to hang with poets, you'll want to be familiar with the structures that have been shaping poetry for a very long time. The third is that form is a shared language. If you start a workshop with people just bringing in poems, that can work, but you won't necessarily have a shared set of reference points or an understanding of what each poet was trying to do. If you start a workshop with shared exercises—if the whole class writes abecedarians, and everyone had to get from A to Z—then you have a place to start every discussion. It's a bit like when you watch a cooking show on television and all the contestants have to make a variation of the same dish. It's much easier to talk to each other about how the croissants came out than for everyone to just cook whatever they were going to make anyway. Which isn't to say you'll never go to a potluck where everyone brings their favorite dish (that sounds like a fun end-of-semester activity actually), but that when you're trying to develop skills together, it helps if everyone has a shared foundation of expectation and possibility.

If you're still with me, let's get started!

1 An Arbitrary Order Still Makes Demands
The Abecedarian

There's no real reason for A to come first in the alphabet. There is a history behind why A is first, but that's not the same as a logical reason. Our letter A evolved over time from other versions of that letter in other writing systems—but does A have to be first? Not at all. And yet, almost all of us learn to sing the alphabet song just as we're starting to learn to read. When we learn to count, it's sort of important that you start with 1, go on to 2, then 3, and so on. Certainly we could start counting with zero and really confuse kids (have *you* ever tried to explain what zero is?), but 1 really is a logical starting place.

A coming first is totally arbitrary. In a much older writing system for the languages that became English, the letter for the *f* sound came first. That writing system is commonly referred to as being made up of runes, and those runes used to share space with Latin letters. That set of letters is known as *futhark*, because those were the first letters in that alphabet (Findell 16), and confidently, they form a word you can say out loud. You can't make a word out of "ABC," so we just say each letter and call them the "ABCs." In fact the word "alphabet" makes more sense when you look at Greek, in which the first two letters are named "alpha" and "beta." There is a lot of variation in terms of how writing has developed in different times and places. Arabic has two ordering systems for its letters. Japanese has two sets of characters for writing—one phonetic and one not. It's easy to think that learning the ABCs is the obvious first step to learning any language, but it's actually pretty specific to English. All phonetic writing systems emerged from a single common ancestor but have diverged pretty widely in how they are deployed and understood.

Another reason we need to know the names of our letters is that our use of Latin letters is only partly phonetic. In Russia, if you ask someone to spell a word, they don't say the names of the letters; they just pronounce each sound very clearly, and that's enough. Other languages that use Latin letters

(French, Spanish, Polish, etc.) often use accents and diacritical marks to make pronunciation match spelling. But in English, we seem pretty committed to an inconsistent use of our letters. There's a Dr. Seuss book called *The Tough Coughs as He Ploughs the Dough* calling attention to the absurdity of "ough" being called upon to make so many different sounds. We don't even agree across the language! Americans write "color," and Brits write "colour." So go ahead and pat yourself on the back for having learned your ABCs and having adjusted to English's highly inconsistent orthography. If you can read this paragraph, you're doing pretty well!

Once you do know the alphabet, you've learned an order, and that order can be used to structure poems. Poems that are structured by the alphabet are known as "abecedarians." The most dense abecedarian would have only twenty-six words—one word for each letter.

Writing an Abecedarian
After beginning, carefully drift evenly forward.
Grief has it's just knowledge. Love makes new
Our preciously quiet receiving. Suffering
Tricks us. Vanity wails xylophonic, you zany.

The most famous of these twenty-six-word poems is Robert Pinsky's "ABC" from his collection *Jersey Rain*. Pinsky adds a symbol, putting an equals sign between the X and the Y, so that he can have a proper sentence at the end. I made up the word "xylophonic"—meaning something that sounds like a xylophone. I could even have gone with "xylophonically" to make it an adverb. It's important to give yourself room to play—the restrictive structure of a poetic form should make you find creative solutions.

Whenever you write an abecedarian, the XYZ is almost always the hardest. It feels like those letters end up at the end of the alphabet because we use them so rarely! It's a good idea, when faced with an abecedarian, to figure out the XYZ first, and then go back to the rest of the poem. If you are at a loss for words, you can google "words that start with X" or—even more fun—you can find an old-fashioned paper dictionary and just look through the X section. One of the things I like about abecedarians is that they always increase my vocabulary. Jessica Greenbaum used "zarfs" for the Z in her abecedarian "A Poem for S." A zarf is a glass cup with a metal frame around it that provides a handle. I have drunk out of many zarfs over the years, but never knew they had a specific name until I read her poem and looked it up. One of my favorite words in English is "antimacassar"—a piece of cloth that you put over the back of a chair that prevents hair oils from staining the chair. It's an oddly specific word for an oddly specific thing, and I encountered it while reading Victorian novels. If you're stuck, try starting your abecedarian with "antimacassar," though the letter A starts so many words that I find students are rarely at a loss at the *beginning* of the alphabet.

Most abecedarians have twenty-six lines, and each line begins with the next letter. Technically, this form of the abecedarian is called an "abecedarius". Here is an abecedarius about writing:

Inspiration
All inspiration comes from
Being pressured to do something
Courageous. What's all this slightly
Deranged emphasis on ordering
Each letter, gaining so much power
From being arranged and passed from
Generation to generation, in a
Harebrained unity that lasts and lasts
Into each new century. Writing
Just has this power to transform
Knowledge, to make it your own, to
Lift the skills from page to hand to
Mind, and what you have done is
New, totally new. You play with
Our shared heritage, with letters
Placed in your hands by those
Questing for a way to capture
Reasons and feelings on the page
Secured there with inky shapes.
Trust that what you need others to
Understand will be seen here, made
Visible as you write the words.
We'll end up here, pen to paper, in
Xanadu (another name for heaven)
You wanted to be a writer? Wow-
Zers! You did it.

The abecedarius has its origins in Hebrew prayer. I was taught that the abecedarius was used for prayers to make sure one didn't get too lost in the joy of song. These were farmers who had to get back to the fields, so the alphabet set a reasonable limit on the length of the poem, which was also a prayer.

Once we have an order, you have built an expectation for your reader. Much of the pleasure of formal poetry is in recognizing the demands and restraints—knowing what has to come next and getting excited by how the writer has fulfilled those expectations. It's a lot more fun to work on formal poems together. Then everyone gets to show off how they solved the problem, and we all get to see how our friends and classmates solved the problem.

One of my favorite forms of the abecedarian is the abecedarian that allows you to stay with one letter and then move on to the next. So you can have as many words that start with A as you need, then words that start with B, and so on. I find that this form is really effective if you know a lot about a particular subject, like superhero movies, dance moves, sports teams, painters, presidents, or anything else. Here's one with film directors:

Filmic Abecedarian with Stutter

Almodóvar's best cuts demonstrate
Everything. Forget Griffith's hits.
How hollow Ingmar, in juxtaposition.
Kubrick? Lang? Muck-abouts.
Not one peer *para Pedro*.
Pedro's questing reveals Spain's terrifying (typifying) universalism.
Vanquishes Wim Wenders.
Xceeds you,
yes you,
Zeferelli.

If you start with the difficulty of finding a good "X" word, you could write one of these poems around tyrants (Xerxes), technology (Xerox), saints (Xavier), cities (Xi'an), goddesses (Xochiquetzal), and so on.

As you get the hang of the abecedarian, you can start creating your own variations. You could start with any letter and then circle back. So let's say your name starts with an "L." You could start your abecedarian with the letter L, go to Z, start again from A, and then end at K. The possibilities really are endless, as long as the alphabet is clearly there. John Deming has pioneered a double abecedarian, in which the first line starts with A but then ends with Z; the second line starts with B and ends with Y, all the way until the final line that starts with Z and ends with A. As long as the alphabet is clearly being used as a structure, you can be as inventive and clever as you want to be.

If you have all been enjoying the abecedarian and would like an additional challenge, try writing an anagram poem or an acrostic. An acrostic is like the abecedarius, but instead of the first letters of each line spelling out the alphabet, they spell out a name or a message. For example, Edgar Allan Poe wrote this poem in response to a poet named Elizabeth who used the initials L. E. L. as her pen name. Poe responds with his own thoughts on love, and the first letter of each line spells out the name "Elizabeth."

An Acrostic

Elizabeth it is in vain you say
"Love not"—thou sayest it in so sweet a way:
In vain those words from thee or L.E.L.
Zantippe's talents had enforced so well:
Ah! if that language from thy heart arise,
Breath it less gently forth—and veil thine eyes.
Endymion, recollect, when Luna tried
To cure his love—was cured of all beside—
His follie—pride—and passion—for he died.

Edgar Allan Poe

Anagrams are when you rearrange the letters to spell a new word. For example, if you take my last name, you can rearrange the letters in "Jason Schneiderman" to spell "Hinderances, no jams," which does not make a lot of sense. But one of my students, who truly loved anagrams, added a word, and "Poet Jason Schneiderman" can be rearranged to "Nascent hope joins dreams." Some names are simple to rearrange, and others take a bit more work. In anagram poems, people often bring back their name, or a variation of their names, to interesting effect. Some names have a lot of anagrams. Henri Cole wrote a poem called "Anagram" in which the letters in his name are rearranged to spell "heron lice," "lion cheer," "I clone her," and "iron leech." See what happens if you try to scramble the letters in your name, or the name of someone you like, love, or admire.

I like to start with abecedarian because we tend not to really think about letters, and even though we all know alphabetical order, we don't necessarily use it to make art. In my classes, there are usually some people who love poetry and feel very comfortable writing poetry, and some people who are very nervous about poetry and find it intimidating. The alphabet lets us all start in a similar place, making poetry out of a shared knowledge we hadn't thought to make art from yet. It's also a thrill to go through the first batch of abecedarian and see how differently each student responds to the same poetic form.

Template

Obviously you already know your ABCs, but having the structure ready for you on the page can make writing so much easier! In each chapter, the template is there to help you remember all the aspects of the form.

A _____
B _____
C _____
D _____
E _____
F _____
G _____
H _____
I _____
J _____
K _____
L _____
M _____
N _____
O _____
P _____
Q _____
R _____
S _____
T _____
U _____
V _____
W _____
X _____
Y _____
Z _____

A Few Hints for Writing the Abecedarian

1. Start with the end. If you can solve the problem of what to do with XYZ, everything else will be easier. I often recommend playing with the "X," so that it might become "X-ceed" or "X-plore." Could "X" become the roman numeral for "10"?
2. Use a subject that will let you use your expertise. For example, if you write about animals, you can also assign an animal to difficult letters. I wrote an abecedarian about film directors, so I could end on "Zeffirelli." In solving the problem of the "x," I advise that a poem about the elements would offer "xenon," a poem about dictators could give you "Xerxes," and a poem about places might yield "Xanadu."
3. Decide how far you can bend the rules. Pinsky allows himself a symbol to get through a particularly rough patch. If you heard the poem out loud, you might be surprised that "e" (since you would say "equals") shows up at the end, but visually (orthographically), the rules are obeyed. Would "X-chromosome" be an acceptable "x" word? My own rule of thumb is that I let myself out of one formal constraint in every formal poem. So I might skip one rhyme in a sonnet, or allow a sestina to have one open space instead of an end word.
4. It's usually easier not to tell a story, but if you are going to use a story, use unnamed characters. If you start with "Andrew bought Carla diamonds," neither name can come back into the poem. Though you could wait for "h" to get to "he/him/her" and "s" for "she" or "t" for "they/them," if you really wanted to use that beginning.

Abecedarian Exercises

1. Write a twenty-six-word abecedarian.
2. Write an abecedarian with names from an area you know a lot about.
3. Come up with your own variation on the abecedarian.
4. Write an abecedarian about food.
5. Write an abecedarian in praise of something or someone you love.

How to Share and Workshop an Abecedarian

1. Always start by asking *how* the alphabet was used. What did the poet do to make the alphabetic order their own?
2. Ask how the hardest letters were used, especially the letter "X." Are there any letters that forced the writer to pick an unusual word, something they wouldn't normally use when writing or speaking?
3. What knowledge did the author bring to the poem? How did they bring something they know that might be specialized or unusual into the poem by using the alphabet?

2 Looking in the Broken Mirror
The Ghazal

The ghazal makes an interesting demand. To write a ghazal, you have to write a poem that approaches a single topic from multiple perspectives. In English language poetry, the poem is usually unified by something. Most commonly, our poems are held together by a speaking voice (a monologue), by a story being told (a narrative), or by an argument being pursued (a meditation). The ghazal shatters those unities. The ghazal is made up of couplets (two-line stanzas), but those couplets are not supposed to flow into each other. Each couplet ends with the same word, so you always have to arrive at the same place, but each couplet is supposed to take a new approach to the thing you are writing about. Agha Shahid Ali, who popularized the formal ghazal in American letters, puts it this way: "One couplet may be comic, another tragic, another romantic, another religious, another political" (2). I often explain the ghazal by saying that it's like looking into a broken mirror—each fragment reflects a different aspect of the thing you're looking at, rather than showing you a single image.

Every ghazal is built around a repeated word. Every couplet will end with that word, and that's usually the subject of the ghazal, and often the title as well. Think hard about the word you're going to have to keep approaching. Most ghazals are five to twelve couplets, so it should be something you can think about in a lot of different ways. We'll start by choosing a word to repeat. I'll be a little on the nose and choose the word "repetition."

    Repetition.

Obviously, the repeating word will repeat. In the first couplet, it ends both lines. In every couplet after, the repeating word will only end the second line. For our first couplet, we'll have to fill in the blanks, but so far we have this:

_____repetition

_____repetition

Now we need a rhyme to go in front of the repeating word. It's important to choose a word that has lots of rhymes. Don't choose "orange" or "silver." I was playing around and settled on "east." But since "repetition" is an abstraction, it turned out to be helpful to use a preposition, so I'm going to go with "-east of." For the first couplet, the rhyme occurs twice:

_____-east of repetition

_____-east of repetition

So now let's write a starting couplet that actually uses words that rhyme:

The ghazal provides a feast of repetition.

It asks you to love the beast of repetition.

It's fun to come up with rhymes from your own thoughts, especially as a class, but you can also use a rhyming dictionary or ask the internet. "East" rhymes with "feast," "priest," "beast," "policed," "greased," "ceased," "Dianne Wiest" (she's an actress your parents liked), "released," and we could keep going! If a lot of rhymes come to mind, that's great. And you can write them down on your paper to get yourself going. If you're writing the poem as a class, it's fun to come up with the repeating word together and then see who can come up with a rhyme that has the most words as you put the rhymes up on the board.

After the first couplet, the rhyme and refrain are only at the end of each couplet. You have a lot of freedom because you have a lot of space before you have to come back to that rhyme and refrain. Usually, a ghazal has five to twelve couplets.

There's one more rule! In the last couplet, you are supposed to refer to yourself. When I'm working with new groups of students, I often have them come up with a group name so that they can address themselves in the final couplet. When addressing yourself, get creative with how to bring yourself into the poem. I used my name twice in this final couplet. I might be

Professor Schneiderman to my students, but when I talk to myself in my head, I'm always just Jason.

Ghazal: Repetition

The ghazal provides a feast of repetition.
It asks you to love the beast of repetition.

Six years old, my British accent dying in
California. Voices lost, east of repetition.

A joke about Carnegie hall: Practice!
Virtuosity rises from the yeast of repetition.

Should you memorize poems? Maybe,
I say. Yes, says the priest of repetition.

Jason, are you ever tired of poems? Never!
But poems end. You are released of repetition.

The ghazal is the oldest poetic form still in use, hundreds of years older than the sonnet. It has roots in Urdu, Hindi, Hebrew, and Arabic. Agha Shahid Ali was very insistent that the word be pronounced "GHUH-zl." The "gh" is sort of like the "kh" at the end of "Bach," but with a "g" being brought back into your throat instead of a "k." Ali described it "as a close relative of the French 'r.'" I tell my students, many of whom try the "gh," that it may be easier to just stick with saying "guzzle" or "huzzle." However, Ali's pronunciation is, in fact, the Urdu pronunciation. Arab speakers pronounce the word "gha-ZAHL" (Hebrew speakers pronounce the word like Arab speakers, but with a slight difference in the "gh" sound that, I am told, exists). My own feeling is that policing the pronunciation of the word "ghazal" should be a low priority. The name is said to originate as an onomatopoeia for the cry a hunted gazelle makes when it has been captured and knows it will die.

The ghazal in most of the world is a sung and a spoken form. When the ghazal is familiar to its listeners, it has a special excitement that builds. Here is Ali's description of the mushaira, or the traditional readings of ghazals: "When the poet recites the first line of a couplet, the audience recites it back to him, and then the poet repeats it, and the audience again follows suit." You can also try this with your students—have them be the audience reciting back the line to one of the students as she reads her ghazal. But while the number of repetitions in the mushaira seems driven by the excitement of the audience (like curtain calls), I would specify how many repetitions you expect. In class, Ali would tell us about what a thrill it was at the readings to get—after many repetitions—to the refrain.

David Jalalel's excellent history of the ghazal traces the emergence of the ghazal to the Umayyad Era, also known as the Second Caliphate (661–750). The two undisputed masters of the ghazal are Hafiz (1325–89), writing in Persian, and Mirza Ghalib (1797–1869), writing in Urdu. There were ghazals in English prior to the 1960s (James Clarence Mangan used the form in the 1920s), but they gained a new prominence when Aijaz Ahmad invited well-known American poets to translate Ghalib's ghazals, in honor of the centenary of his death. Most of these translations are in free verse, and Adrienne Rich's "Ghazals (Homage to Ghalib)" set the American model for the ghazal. Rich was attracted to the disjointed quality of the form, which allowed her to express a certain kind of rupture she felt in the world around her. In the 1990s, Agha Shahid Ali began to work on bringing the formal rules of the ghazal back into English and encouraging poets to write what he called "real Ghazals." The rules that I've presented here are all based on the template provided by Ali in his 2001 anthology, *Ravishing Disunities: Real Ghazals in English*, an impressive collection of formal ghazals. This anthology remains the best source for structured ghazals in English. Ali's own ghazals were posthumously published in the book *Call Me Ishmael Tonight*.

Ali writes that the classic ghazal is unified by a longing for the beloved, and many of his ghazals achieve this unity. The mood of the Urdu and Persian ghazal is described by Ali as "melancholic and amorous." And while there are certainly melancholic ghazals in English, I find that the ghazals I gravitate toward tend to be clever, full of impish humor and mischief. Without melody, the ghazal in English often takes a playful approach to the refrain, trying to see how many ways it can be reinvented and reframed.

Ghazal Template

_____rhyme refrain
_____rhyme refrain

_____
_____rhyme refrain

_____
_____rhyme refrain

_____
_____rhyme refrain

_____
_____rhyme refrain

Additional Rules and Information

1. The rhyme is also called the qafia. The refrain is also called the radif. The first couplet has a special name too: the matla. The last couplet is called the makhta.
2. The ghazal should be five to twelve couplets long.

3. Address yourself in the final couplet, or at the very least, use your own name. If you are writing as a group, use your group name, or come up with one.
4. Each couplet should make sense on its own.

A Few Hints for Writing a Ghazal

1. It helps to have something that is important but still kind of new to you. Like let's say you have to move to California (as I did as a child), and people keep talking about it, but you aren't sure what it means to you. Try writing a ghazal with "California" as the repeating word. Or you just discovered a new style of music or art and want to write about it.
2. Try to use lots of different modes for the couplets. I like to have a couplet with a factoid, a couplet that recounts a story, a couple that makes an argument, and so on. If each couplet is very similar, try to mix it up and come up with other ways to end on the same refrain.

Ghazal Exercises

1. Write a ghazal together, but do it in two ways. First, come up with the refrain and rhyme together and write the stanzas as a group. Next, come up with the first stanza (the matla) together and then have each student write the couplet they want to add to the poem on their own. Then decide on what order to put the couplets once everyone has finished.
2. Denver Butson came up with a form for his poem "Drowning Ghazals," in which he took a line from a poem and then used that line to establish his ghazal. So if you used Shakespeare's "There is nothing either good or bad but thinking makes it so". You might use "makes it so" as the reframing, and "-inking" as the rhyme.
3. Come up with a rhyme and refrain, but then swap with someone else so that you have to write to the other person's interest.

How to Share and Workshop a Ghazals

1. The ghazal is "modular," meaning that you can basically treat the couplets like LEGO blocks that you can move around. Ask how the order of the couplets is working. Could they go in a different order? Why?
2. The ghazal takes a kaleidoscopic view of whatever is mentioned in the refrain. What is the image that emerges? After approaching the refrain in a different way in each couplet, what aspects of the topic have been revealed?

3 The Divided Self Is a Field of Play
The Sonnet

Sonnets are a very big deal. If people have only ever heard of one poetic form, it's usually the sonnet. In the days of apprenticeship, where learning a trade meant watching an accomplished craftsman work until the apprentice knew how to ply the craft by himself, the apprenticeship ended with the young person creating a "masterpiece." The idea of the masterpiece was that it contained all the techniques that had been learned, but also that the apprentice was now a master. So if someone had been apprenticed to a clockmaker, they would make one clock showing off every single technique they'd learned. For a lot of poets, writing a sonnet is a key part of their development and gives them access to that tradition of English language writing. A sonnet often lets a poet show off what they can do. Sonnets can act as a kind of masterpiece for poets. In an essay about the sonnet in the United States, Dora Malech and Laura Smith note that American poets "often write as if they are asserting their right to belong" (1).

Phillis Levin provides a remarkable history of the sonnet in her anthology *The Penguin Book of the Sonnet*. Sonnets were the first poems in English that were written to be spoken aloud instead of sung to a melody (Levin xli). Before the sonnet, there wasn't a clear distinction between song lyrics and poetry, but the sonnet essentially established poetry in the way that we understand it now. It's also the case that the sonnet—which began in Italy in the 1200s—reached Britain just as Modern English was emerging in the 1500s. The earlier forms of English (Middle English and Old English) had different rules for their poems, so when you write a sonnet, you're basically going back to the origins of the English language as we speak it, and the origins of poetry as we understand it. The sonnet has been evolving from the very moment of its creation. The form is credited to Giacomo de Lentino, but his creation used repeated words rather than rhymes (Levin 337), though rhymes soon replaced the repetitions.

Sonnets also mark a big change in the way that people in Europe understood themselves. A big thing that distinguishes Medieval Europe from the Renaissance was what we would basically call "psychology." We think of ourselves as being kind of confusing. We are full of contradictions, and we often do things that we know are bad—like staying up playing video games when we know we have to be up for school the next day—because we have desires that we can't quite reconcile. We often feel two things that don't make sense together. You might love and hate a person at the same time. Or you know you should be doing your homework, but you really want to keep scrolling social media (or reading that novel). That sense of ourselves as divided and full of contradictory feelings and impulses started around the same time that the sonnet came to England. Before that, people were definitely conflicted, but it wasn't complicated in the same way. For Medieval people, you have a bad impulse to have fun and good impulse to work, and sometimes one wins, and sometimes the other wins. But for modern people (and the Renaissance is also called "the early modern period"), we are responding to past traumas and experiences in ways that make us mysterious to ourselves. The sonnet is built around a turn, around feeling some kind of division in our own feelings that need to be explored. The sonnet enacts that new experience of the self.

To learn how to write sonnets, first we have to learn to read a rhyme scheme. Just like your camp counselor told you not to swim alone, rhymes can't happen without pairs. A rhyme scheme tells you where the rhymes should go. Let's start with four rhyming words, and for convenience, we'll put them on their own lines:

Apace

Far

Place

Mar

"Apace" is our first word, and the first letter is A. So the "-ace" sound will be A. "Far" does not rhyme with "Apace," so we'll go to the next letter, B. Now any word ending with the sound "-ar" will be B. Place brings us back to "-ace," so we use an A, and then "Mar" ends with "-ar," so we go back to B. Our rhyme scheme looks like this:

A

B

A

B

So let's say we get to the next four end words:

Wag

Tree

Bag

Thee

"Wag" doesn't end with "-ace" or "-ar", so we'll go to the next letter: C. And then "tree" is also a new ending sound. So we'll move on to D. You should be getting the pattern by now, which is

C

D

C

D

You may have guessed by some of the old-timey words (we don't use "thee" anymore) that I'm actually teaching you the rhyme scheme using a fairly old poem. These ending words are from a poem by Sir Walter Ralegh, and it's a warning to his son. It's usually titled "To His Son," but back when he was writing, poets didn't title their own poems, and the editors would often put the title *after* the poem. Weird, right? Things change.

Let's look at the whole poem, and then we'll go back and finish the rhyme scheme. I'm putting the ending rhyme sounds in bold, but don't do that when you write your own poems. I just want you to see the rhyming sounds very clearly.

To His Son

Three things there be that prosper up ap**ace**
And flourish, whilst they grow asunder f**ar**,
But on a day, they meet all in one pl**ace**,
And when they meet, they one another m**ar**;
And they be these: the wood, the weed, the w**ag**.
The wood is that which makes the gallow tr**ee**;
The weed is that which strings the hangman's b**ag**;
The wag, my pretty knave, betokeneth th**ee**.
Mark well, dear boy, whilst these assemble n**ot**,
Green springs the tree, hemp grows, the wag is w**ild**,
But when they meet, it makes the timber r**ot**,
It frets the halter, and it chokes the ch**ild**.
Then bless thee, and beware, and let us pr**ay**
We part not with thee at this meeting d**ay**.

Walter Ralegh

This is a super dark poem. The "wood" is a gallows—a structure for executing someone by hanging. The "weed" is a rope—used to hang someone to be executed. And "wag" is his son's head on his neck. A "wag" is slang for a young man, and not too far from the word swagger. One of the weirdest things to me about this poem is that the speaker is just like "hey kiddo, don't get executed" but gives him zero advice about how not to run afoul of the law. In the 1500s, a lot of poets were also diplomats, which is why they were reading sonnets in continental Europe and bringing the form back to Britain. But we'll get back to the rhyme scheme which is

    A

    B

    A

    B

    C

    D

    C

D

E

F

E

F

G

G

Another thing to note is that while "thee" and "thou" are forms of "you" that didn't survive to the present day, they are actually more intimate than "you." "Thee" is the form you would use for a pet or a child—it's like calling someone by their first name. Because as contemporary speakers of English, we only see thee and thou in Shakespeare and the Bible, we often conclude that "thee" must be very formal, but it's actually what you use for someone you love and know well. If you use "thee/thou" in prayer, it's because God is supposed to be as close to you as a parent. "Thee" and "thou" should not be read as distant or formal, but intimate and loving. If you start reading sonnets, you'll come across a lot of "thee"s and "thou"s, so it's good to know that they are usually to people that the writer feels very close to.

The form we just looked at is known as the English sonnet, or the Shakespearean sonnet, even though it was around before Shakespeare! In the English sonnet, the turn often comes just before the final couplet. Couplet rhyme in English often has the effect of closure or making things feel sealed and complete. There is usually a smaller turn somewhere after line 8.

Sonnets have a very wide array of forms. Most forms are fairly rigid, but the sonnet has been evolving as long as it has been around. The form is said to have been invented by one person: Giacomo da Lentini, a lawyer in the court of Frederick the Second. In Lentini's creation, there weren't rhymes at all, but repeated end words, like in a sestina! Later those became rhymes. When the sonnet moved to England, a version that we call the English (or Shakespearean) sonnet emerged, presumably because the rhyme scheme of the Italian sonnet is so hard to pull off in English, where there are fewer rhymes. When Alexander Pushkin was writing a novel in verse in Russian, he developed his own version of the sonnet that was a hybrid of the English and the Italian sonnet. John Milton made a longer sonnet with extra tails, called a "caudated sonnet" ("cauda" is Latin for "tail"). Gerard Manley Hopkins created a shorter sonnet called the "curtal sonnet."

The two most common forms of the sonnet are the Italian and the English. I wanted to start with the English sonnet because I feel like it's a bit more natural for us when we are writing. I also wanted to start with a poem that's not a love poem—or maybe is a love poem, but not a romantic love poem but rather a parental love poem. Let's look at another famous poem to get the rhyme scheme for the Italian sonnet. As you know, lots of sonnets are love poems, often exploring the question of what it means to love someone else. This poem is by Elizabeth Barrett Browning. She wrote love poems to her husband Robert Browning, who was also a poet. She married him against her father's wishes, so there was a forbidden quality to their love. Her love poems were highly celebrated and still are.

Sonnet 43

How do I love thee? Let me count the ways.
I love thee to the depth and breadth and height
My soul can reach, when feeling out of sight
For the ends of being and ideal grace.
I love thee to the level of every day's
Most quiet need, by sun and candle-light.
I love thee freely, as men strive for right.
I love thee purely, as they turn from praise.
I love thee with the passion put to use
In my old griefs, and with my childhood's faith.
I love thee with a love I seemed to lose
With my lost saints. I love thee with the breath,
Smiles, tears, of all my life; and, if God choose,
I shall but love thee better after death.

Elizabeth Barrett Browning

A

B

B

A

A
B
B
A
C
D
C
D
C
D

You can see right away that this rhyme scheme only gets to D. Every rhyme gets used three to five times! In the Shakespearean sonnet, you get to G, and every rhyme only comes back once. You can also see how the poem shifts after the octave—or the first eight lines. The octave is all about figuring out how she can describe the love she feels. The sestet—or the last grouping of six lines—is all about what that love has meant. The love she feels for her husband has made up for a sad childhood, for losing her faith in her religion, and she hopes that she can love him even more in the afterlife.

When starting a sonnet, the most important thing is to have some sense of division. The subject has to be something that you're conflicted about, so that the poem can give you the space to write about the divisions you're experiencing. An English sonnet is easier since there are fewer rhymes, but many poets have preferred the Italian sonnet for its complexity and more demanding rhyme scheme. Also, an English sonnet has a hard turn into the final couplet, while an Italian sonnet has a softer turn into the final sestet after the first eight lines.

Gerard Manley Hopkins invented a smaller, truncated sonnet called the "curtal sonnet." Hopkins was a Jesuit priest who destroyed a lot of his earlier poems because he felt that they were not in line with his calling as a religious man. Faith is a very common theme in his poems, and this poem is no exception.

Pied Beauty

Glory be to God for dappled things—
    For skies of couple-colour as a brinded cow;
        For rose-moles all in stipple upon trout that swim;
Fresh-firecoal chestnut-falls; finches' wings;
    Landscape plotted and pieced—fold, fallow, and plough;
        And all trades, their gear and tackle and trim.

All things counter, original, spare, strange;
    Whatever is fickle, freckled (who knows how?)
        With swift, slow; sweet, sour; adazzle, dim;

He fathers-forth whose beauty is past change:
    Praise Him.

Gerard Manley Hopkins

An interesting feature of the curtal sonnet is that the final line only has two syllables, and both are stressed. Two stressed syllables together are called a spondee.

    A
    B
    C
    A
    B
    C
    D
    B
    C
    D
    C (spondee line)

I invented a sonnet form called the Schneiderman sonnet, which is a couplet sonnet, but using homophones instead of rhymes. It has not caught on, but I'm still working on it! Almost all scholars agree that the most important thing about the sonnet is the turn, or volta. As long as your sonnet enacts the divided self, you are clearly in sonnet territory. I'm a stickler about the fourteen lines, with all due respect to the caudated and curtal sonnet, but you should know that the sonnet continues to evolve to meet the needs of the poets working in the form—and those poets now include you! I am a fan of the Pushkin sonnet, which Aleksander Pushkin created to write his novel in verse *Yevgeny Onegin*. A lot of the pleasures of the Russian poetry get lost in translation, so the poem has never been very popular outside of the Russian-speaking world. The Pushkin sonnet has been popular, though, and its form is a hybrid of the Italian and the English sonnet.

The Legend of Alexander Pushkin

He died in a duel he ought not have fought,
The first Russian writer to write in Russian.
He loved his wife though she loved him not.
The Tsar himself was Pushkin's bludgeon.
His sideburns were famous, and still are.
In the Slavic sky, he's the brightest star.
He hated his life in the great king's court,
Asked for release, but the Tsar did thwart
His efforts to leave, and kept him near,
Mostly for his wife, though he loved his verse
And wanted him write the very first
Account of his life, with not a jot of fear
That Pushkin might refuse or leave.
Then the duel. His death. And we still grieve.

A

B

A

B

C
C
D
D
E
F
F
E
G
G

Vikram Seth used the Pushkin sonnet as the stanza form for his novel in verse, *The Golden Gate*.

You will notice a lot of "ABAB" and "ABBA" rhymes in the various forms. In Italian, the ABAB rhyme is called "rima alternata" or "alternating rhyme," while the "ABBA" structure is called "rima baciata" or "kissing rhyme." I love the idea of the embedded rhyming couplet as the two rhymes kissing.

As you start writing your sonnets, you are entering a tradition that is centuries old and is often synonymous with poetry itself. The sonnet form forces compression: you have to take a huge concern and fit it into just fourteen lines. The sonnet allows you to handle the really big stuff on a very small scale.

Templates

The Italian Sonnet

A
B
B
A
A
B
B
A

C   C
D   D
C or E
D   C
C   D
D   E

The sestet can be arranged in almost any order as long as there are only two or three rhymes.

The English Sonnet

A

B

A

B

C

D

C

D

E

F

E

F

G

G

The Pushkin Sonnet

A

B

A

B

C

C

D

D

E

F

F

E

G

G

The Curtal Sonnet

A

B

C

A

B

C

D

B

C

D

C (spondee line)

There are many forms of the sonnet—the *Penguin Book of the Sonnet* presents almost twenty variations of the form.

A Few Hints for Writing Sonnets

1. The sonnet is usually about some kind of division.
2. Try different rhyme schemes to see which one fits you best.

Exercises

1. Take the rhyme scheme from a sonnet in the public domain (Shakespeare is always safely in the public domain) and use the poem's end words. So if you took Sonnet 116, you would write a sonnet using the same rhymes. Make sure that you give credit to the author whose end words you used—and if the poem is under copyright, make sure you contact the author and get permission before you publish it.
2. Sonnets are often in conversation with other sonnets. Write a sonnet about another sonnet.
3. Sonnets are often portraits. Write a sonnet portrait of one of your favorite authors.
4. Write a sonnet riddle in which the octave poses a question and the sestet answers.

How to Share and Workshop a Sonnet

Start discussing a sonnet by looking at the division. Where is the turn? What is the difference between the sonnet before the turn and after?

4 Satellites and Snowballs
Writing the Villanelle

The very first essay I ever wrote about teaching form was about the villanelle. The villanelle is built around two rhymes that run through the poem and two lines that are repeated across the stanzas. Every villanelle has a circular motion. It's like being on a carousel or a ferris wheel—you keep passing the same starting point. Some villanelles are like satellites going around the earth, and each time you get to the repeating line, you end up in the same place. But some villanelles are like snowballs, picking up size as they roll downhill, with the repeating lines gathering more and more force as you go. Like the ghazal, you need something that bears repeating, but this time it has to be two full lines, not just a single word. Let's take our first stanza.

> Every person must love in their own time.
>
> We are born to our parents, loved unknowns.
>
> When people love, their feelings rhyme.

We can see that this is the rhyme scheme:

> A
>
> B
>
> A

But we're going to add a number to indicate that the entire line repeats. So it will actually be

> A1
>
> B
>
> A2

The second stanza will end by repeating the first line:

> A
>
> B
>
> A1

So let's look at our second stanza:

> As children we play in the dirt and grime.
>
> We play near danger in our safe homes.
>
> Every person must love in their own time.

The third stanza will end on the third line from the first stanza, or the second repeating line.

> Our bodies betray us, changing on a dime.
>
> We see friends anew, feel it in our bones.
>
> When people love, their feelings rhyme.

Verses four and five repeat that pattern:

> A
>
> B
>
> A1
>
> A
>
> B
>
> A2

And then the final stanza brings back both of the repeating lines for a four-line poem ender.

A
B
A1
A2

So let's see the whole poem:

Villanelle of Human Time

Every person must love in their own time.
We are born to our parents, loved unknowns.
When people love, their feelings rhyme.

As children we play in the dirt and grime.
We play near danger in our safe homes.
Every person must love in their own time.

Our bodies betray us, changing on a dime.
We see friends anew, feel it in our bones.
When people love, their feelings rhyme.

Their future becomes a hill to climb.
It's the same song, but we hear new tones.
Every person must love in their own time.

Children are born. It seems a crime
How fast they grow into a world their own.
When people love, their feelings rhyme.

When they see us as old, we feel in our prime.
We hold each others hand, prepare the stones.
Every person must love in their own time.
When people love, their feelings rhyme.

To me, this is a satellite villanelle. We return to the same two lines, but they always mean the same thing. Like astronauts in orbit watching the sunrise every couple of hours, the reader of a villanelle keeps coming back to the same line, with the same meaning. We follow the cycle of life, but each time, we return to the idea of finding love and being in our time. The most famous satellite villanelle in English might be Dylan Thomas's "Do Not Go Gentle." That poem has repeating lines begging his father to fight for his life. Let's try a snowball villanelle. When a snowball rolls downhill, it picks up more snow. Each time the same spot comes up, the snowball grows in size and heft. In a snowball villanelle, the lines take on different meanings as they return with a new intensity.

Criminal Villanelle

Let's return to the scene of the crime.
A chalk outline erased, an empty street.
Is it true all wounds are healed by time?

Reactions need the right enzyme.
I am alone here on my own two feet.
Let's return to the scene of the crime.

We vowed we'd be together a full lifetime,
And then you swore that we'd never again meet.
Is it true all wounds are healed by time?

Alone, I come back to where where I'm
Able to remember how our love was sweet.
Let's return to the scene of the crime.

I feel like a cut exposed to salt or lime.
How can I heal a cut that's ragged, not neat?
Is it true all wounds are healed by time?

I feel so stuck here, the same old chime
Ringing repeatedly. Feet! Be fleet!
Let's (not) return to the scene of the crime.
Is it true all wounds are healed by time?

I call this a snowball villanelle because the meanings of the repeating lines keep changing and coming back in new ways. At first the crime seems like an actual crime, but then it becomes clear that it's a metaphor, and that the crime is really a breakup that the speaker can't move on from. As we move through the lines, it becomes clear that the speaker wants to move on. I even allowed a small change in the last stanza to show that now the speaker wants to stop dwelling on the past. The final question is now hopeful instead of futile.

Unlike the pantoum or sestina, which can progress with a modicum of backtracking, the villanelle is anchored to its beginning. The first stanza determines the ending of each successive stanza, which means that the poet can never stray more than two lines from his first assertion. This circularity lends the villanelle an obsessive quality and forces the poet to fixate on a single idea, claim, or mood. Resisting progression, the form demands that exploration be inward, that the mood or fear or desire laid out in the initial stanza expand in understanding and in texture—rather than in narrative stages.

Most students find the villanelle an oddity upon first encounter—awkward and artificial, an exercise in stagnation designed to frustrate. Introducing students to the villanelle has helped me to analyze the form more thoroughly and to discover two distinct ways in which it unfolds—as a satellite or as a snowball. A satellite's path is constant. A satellite falls at the same curve as the curve of the planet it orbits, maintaining a consistent distance from the planet. I like to compare the circular motion of villanelles that remain static in meaning to satellites. The repeating lines of a satellite villanelle remain equidistant (in tone and theme) from the original subject. The subject is explored or expanded with each stanza's newly introduced lines, but the significance revolves around a stable site of obsession or fixation. A snowball villanelle lets the repeating lines gain significance and take on new meanings as the poem moves forward like a snowball picking up snow as it rolls down a mountain.

Template

A1_____

B_____

A2_____

A_____

B_____

A1_____

A_____

B_____

A2_____

A_____

B_____

A1_____

A_____

B_____

A2_____

A_____

B_____

A1_____

A2_____

Note: letters indicate rhymes, while a letter followed by a number indicates a repeating line.

A Few Hints for Writing a Villanelle

1. The repeating lines have to be fairly compelling. They need to be worth repeating, and ideally, they can have slightly different meanings depending on the context.
2. As you draft a villanelle, feel free to keep adjusting the rhyme and the repeating lines.
3. Try to write a snowball villanelle where the meaning of the repeating line can change or take on more power.
4. Look for words with a lot of rhymes so that you have some freedom to write as you go.
5. Allow a few small changes in the repeating lines.

Villanelle Exercises

1. Choose the repeating lines as a class and then have everyone write a different villanelle with those lines.
2. Find a quote you love (from a poem or novel or speech) and use it as one of the repeating lines. Make sure to give credit!
3. Write a villanelle that returns to a powerful memory.
4. Write a villanelle about an animal.

How to Share and Workshop a Villanelle

1. Always start with the repeating lines and how they change or grow as they repeat.
2. How does the poem achieve its full meaning through repetition?
3. Consider the rhymes and how the word choices have shaped the poem.

5 **An Obsession Is a Tether**
The Sestina

Let's do a little math! Do you remember how to find the area of a square? That one should be pretty easy. You just multiply the length of any side by itself, since the sides of any square are all the same length. So if you have a square with two-inch sides, you multiply two inches by two inches and find that you have a square with an area of four square inches. If you want to find the area of a triangle, you multiply the width times the height, and then divide by two. If you want to make a square and a triangle with the same area, it's pretty easy to do. Any triangle that's two inches wide and four inches tall will have an area of four square inches, just like that square.

But what if you want to make a square and a circle with the same area? The area of a circle is calculated using the radius, since a circle has no sides (or more accurately, has only one side). To find the area of a circle, you multiply the radius by itself and then by pi. But pi is a weird number. It's a ratio that won't resolve. Mathematicians in the ancient world were very bothered by this truth: it's impossible to make a square and a circle of the EXACT same area because pi is an irrational number. This problem was called "squaring the circle," and no one can create a square and circle with the exact same area, even if you can get very very close.

But you can square the circle in poetry. And that brings us to the sestina.

The sestina is built around six end words that repeat six times. You have a perfect square in that six times six (6×6 or 6^2). But what about the circle? Well, the order in which the end words repeat is circular. Let's look at how this works. We start with six end words:

A

B

C

D

E

F

And we start our spiral at the bottom.

Our second stanza will start with F. Then we go up to the top.

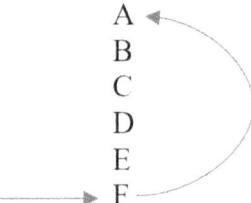

So the second stanza will start with F and then go to A. We spiral back down to E.

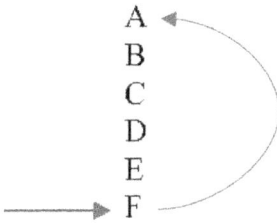

And we can complete the spiral to find the order for the second stanza.

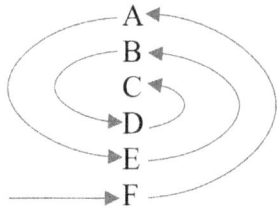

So stanza two will look like this:

F

A

E

B

D

C

This pattern is called "retrogradatio cruciata" (Latin for "cross-wise regression"). Each stanza is shaped by the one before it. So we do the same thing with stanza 2 to get stanza 3. So here are our arrows to show the cross-wise regression for stanza 2:

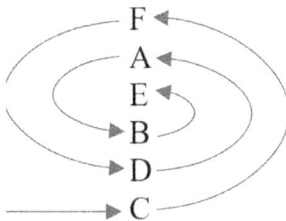

And so our stanza three will look like this:

C

F

D

A

B

E

This goes on for six stanzas. If you had a seventh stanza, it would return to the original pattern of ABCDEF.

Once you have your six stanzas, there is one more stanza, with only three lines. This stanza is called the envoi, and all six end words appear, with three at the end of the line, and three in the middle. I like this particular pattern because it brings us back to the ABCDEF that we would find if we continued with spiraling six-line stanzas:

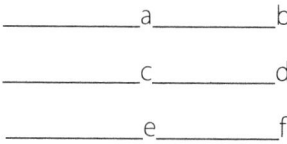

The appeal of this envoi pattern is obvious—the return to the original order is pleasing and tidy. Sir Philip Sidney used this particular envoi pattern in his poem "Sestina," written in 1593. However, the envoi pattern from the earliest sestina, Arnaut Daniel's "Lo ferm voler" follows this pattern.

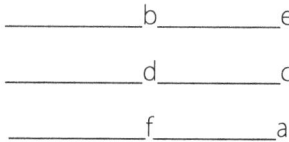

Daniel is often credited with having invented the form in the twelfth century, and this pattern of the envoi is often seen as the "correct" form. Ezra Pound also used this version for his "Sestina: Altaforte" from 1909, and Pound's sestina is often seen as having revived interest in the form in the twentieth century. Many poets skip the envoi altogether, or make up their own patterns out of the end words.

Sestinas require a very particular kind of obsession. The end words have to keep coming back, so you can never stray too far from the vocabulary you have chosen for the teleutons (or end words). Here is a sestina that follows the form we just explored.

Tetherball

> Sestinas always make me think of tether
> Ball, an old fashioned game from last century
> With a ball on a string that you had to wind
> Around a pole in your direction. I was afraid

Of the ball. I always thought it was going
To hit me in the face and break my nose.

Sestinas are a great form for poets with a nose
For repetitions. What else can securely tether
You to an obsession, that just keeps going
Around and around. It's been centurie-
S that poets have been fascinated. Afraid
Of not living up to the form. Or letting the wind

Out of your sails, the form going flat, wind-
Ing up a toy car that can't race, losing by a nose
To anything faster, and always being afraid
That what we write won't be enough to tether
Our reputations to earth. I'm in my second century,
Which feels strange, but that's time: Going

Always forward, never back. I'm not going
To complain about how now is not winding
Up to be any good. Or how this century
Is all self exposure, when last century, nosy
Journalists had to figure it all out, but now we tether
Ourselves by revealing all on social media, afraid

That it is the death of us, but also afraid
Not to see and be seen. Everyone always says we're going
To a worse place than we were, that we tether
Ourselves to the worst leaders, the wind
Always blowing in a bad direction, our noses
Full of the scent of an even worse century

On the horizon. But sestinas will live into a new century,
As long as you write one, there's no need to be afraid

That it's a lost as my childhood playground, noses
Out of joint. The past is always there, but people are going
Into the future, carried on the powerful wind
That reminds us the sestina will always provide a tether.

Release the tether! We're so far into the century
But the wind is still blowing in a way that makes me afraid.
I'm OK not knowing where I'm going. I follow my nose.

Sestinas have been very popular in the last hundred years or so. John Ashbery and his fellow poets of the New York School loved writing sestinas, often giving each other challenges for what to include in them. "Sestinas are easy to write...," John Ashbery asserted in a letter to Kenneth Koch. "After the first stanza they practically write themselves, as if a bicycle, which was hard to pump at first, ended up by pushing your feet with the pedals" (Lehman).

Sestinas also lend themselves to variation. This spiraling structure repetitions, called "retrogradatio cruciata" works great with six, but you can really use it with any number. Marie Ponsot reduced the number of teleutons to three and came up with the tritina, which follows this form:

1

2

3

3

1

2

2

3

1

1----2----3

Virtual School Tritina
Once the bell rang and class
Was over. The day ended
And home we went. But now

Anywhere is everywhere. Now,
We can log in, a virtual class
From home, But if the end

Isn't leaving, does class end?
I feel trapped in an endless now,
As I teach on screen the class.

The class that never ends now.

You could also expand. The "double sestina" can refer to a sestina that goes on for twelve stanzas (with six end words). Charles Algernon Swinburne wrote a sestina with twelve end words, spiraling across twelve stanzas, ending with a six-line envoi, making his poem "The Complaint of Lisa" 150 lines! My students often try their luck with pentinas (five end words), septinas (seven end words), and so on. I often ask students to come up with variations, and I've had classes where ten students came up with their own variations and none of them overlapped! One of my favorite variations is the "shrinking sestina," invented by Miller Williams. In a shrinking sestina, the last verse has only one word per line, meaning that you can start with a six-word sentence as your final stanza and then work backward. In a shrinking sestina, the sixth stanza has one word per line, the fifth stanza has two words per line, and so on.

Part of what keeps the sestina so exciting and various is that idea of how the words generate their own pattern, and how this idea of squaring the circle is at the center of the form. Margaret Spanos explains: "The traditional symbolic import of squaring the circle involves the union of the cosmic symbols of heaven (circle) and earth (square) in a true coincidence of opposites: a synthesis in a higher sphere of reality. Its purpose was to achieve a unity in the material world which transcended the obstacles of matter." Keeping in mind the spiral of the sestina lets you tumble forth into a field of play that determines its own path forward.

Sestina Template

A Diagram of the Sestina

    a

    b

    c

    d

    e

    f

    f

    a

    e

    b

    d

    c

    c

    f

    d

    a

    b

    e

e
c
b
f
a
d

d
e
a
c
f
b

b
d
f
e
c
a

envoi:

_____b_____e   or   _____a_____b
_____d_____c   _____c_____d
_____f_____a   _____e_____f

or other variations (including omission)

A Few Hints for Writing Sestinas

1. Start with the envoi, and then choose your end words from the envoi.
2. Tell a story! Sestinas can sometimes just keep going over the same territory, so having a narrative can create forward thrust.
3. Choose words that have multiple meanings like "bug" (annoy, insect, error . . .) or "frame" so that you can bring back the same end word with multiple meanings.

Exercises

1. Share end words. Come up with end words for the class and have everyone write their own poem using the same end words.
2. Come up with your own variation of the sestina.
3. Write a sestina about a historical figure.
4. Write a shrinking sestina, like Miller Williams's.
5. Write a sestina that tells a story about something that has happened many times.
6. Use end words that could mean a lot of different things.
7. Write a sestina like James Merrill's "Tomorrows" with the end words "one," "two," "three," "four," "five," and "six."

How to Share and Workshop a Sestina

1. Focus on what the end words are doing and how they come back.
2. Consider how the sestina enacts obsessive thinking.
3. Look at how the end words are used differently as they return.

6 One Step Forward, Two Steps Back
The Pantoum

Reading a pantoum is a bit like walking down a spiral staircase. Writing a pantoum is more like playing a game of pick-up sticks. The poem can be of any length and is composed of four-line stanzas, or quatrains, where the second and fourth lines of each stanza become the first and third lines of the next stanza. New lines are written to fill in the rest of the stanza. Since each line of the poem is repeated, every line has to be worth repeating. But the repetition also requires that each line be modular; it has to fit in more than one place. So let's start with our first stanza, remembering that unlike the villanelle, where two lines will repeat over and over again, we're going to have to repeat every single line, but only once.

> Every day I make my bed.
>
> Every morning I make my coffee.
>
> I dress and start over again.
>
> Leaving the house I'll come back to.

The second stanza will use the second and fourth lines as the first and third lines of the next stanza like this.

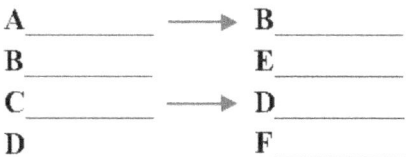

So our second stanza will have to use the second and fourth lines

>Every morning I make my coffee.
>
>_____.
>
>Leaving the house I'll come back to.
>
>_____.

So now we have to fill in those lines:

>Every day I make my bed.
>Every morning I make my coffee.
>I dress and start over again.
>Leaving the house I'll come back to.

>Every morning I make my coffee.
>Wondering that I manage it every day.
>Leaving the house I'll come back to
>The train I take is mostly full.

The third stanza is formed in the same way as the second stanza:

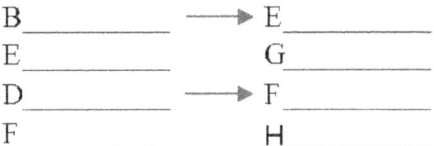

The third stanza builds the same way from the second stanza:

Every morning I make my coffee.

Wondering that I manage it every day.

Leaving the house I'll come back to

The train I take is mostly full.

Wondering that I manage it every day.

I make it to class and sit in my chair.

The train I take is mostly full,

The same at night as in morning.

We keep going until we finally bring back the two lines from the first stanza that have not been repeated yet. The third line from the first stanza becomes the second line, and then the first line becomes the last line.

Villanelle of the Daily Routine

Every day I make my bed.

Every morning I make my coffee.

I dress and start over again.

Leaving the house I'll come back to.

Every morning I make my coffee.

Wondering that I manage it every day.

Leaving the house I'll come back to,

The train I take is mostly full.

Wondering that I manage it every day

I take my place at my desk to work.

The train I take is mostly full
In the night as it was in morning.

I take my place at my desk to work
The work is endless, never done.
In the night as it was in morning,
In my pajamas, the work piled up.

The work is endless, never done.
I wish my home was only calm.
In my pajamas, the work piled up.
Sleeping till waking my only break.

I wish my home was only calm.
I dress and start over again.
Sleeping till waking my only break.
Every day I make my bed.

The movement of a pantoum tends toward either dreamlike wandering or dogged problem-solving. In the first case, the pantoum seems to stray about, to meander over a landscape made only of digressions. When the poem returns to its beginning, the dreamer rediscovers his or her original position. In dogged, problem-solving pantoums, there's an analytic mind at work, and the repetitions feel like evidence under constant review (like the clues on a cop show). The movement of a poem is like a DNA strand, the double helix making new meanings as the lines return.

The pantoum is a very demanding form. I started by saying that reading a pantoum is like walking down a spiral staircase. You keep looping back, but you also make progress—you descend in place. You can also get a bit dizzy.

I love repetitions, and this is the most demanding of the repetition forms. As you revise your pantoums, you'll see how language needs to be manipulated, not just written.

Template

A pantoum can be any length, but the first and third lines (A and C) will always come back as the fourth and second lines of the last stanza. Whatever line begins the poem will also end the poem.

A Few Hints for Writing a Pantoum

1. The first and last lines are the same, so try to choose a first line that will resonate when you arrive there at the end.
2. If you tell a story, make sure that the ending and the beginning look similar.
3. The Pantoum is great for dream logic or associations.
4. When you write the pantoum, let things change or move around as you go. Don't get too attached to any particular arrangement.

Exercises

1. Write a pantoum that explains how you feel about writing poetry.
2. Use a line from a news article as your first line to get the poem started.
3. Check your text messages or emails and use a line to get started.
4. Take a line from another poem you've written to start your pantoum.

How to Share and Workshop a Pantoum

1. Start by discussing how the first line returns as the final line. How has that idea deepened or changed as the poem moved forward?
2. What opportunities are there for the lines to change or take on new meanings as the poem moves forward?
3. What could be done with the syntax to let parts of the repeated lines to make new and surprising sentences.

7 Write What You See
The Ekphrastic Poem

Some writers love to write. Some writers love having written. But all writers seem to complain about how long writing takes, and the vast majority of writers find themselves procrastinating while they wait for inspiration to strike. If you've spent time with writers, you'll know that they spend a lot of time focused on the act of writing. Lots of writers actually have little signs over their desks with a picture of a cute cat and the phrase "You should be writing but here you are looking at a cat." I know one writer who motivated himself by having a sign on his desk reminding him that his arch-rival was writing, so he should be too. Maybe in the future, we'll have signs that say "You could be feeding your ideas into ChatGPT but instead you're looking at this cat." For now, I'll just assume you're like a lot of writers, and sometimes you'd like to write something, but you do not have anything to write about.

Good news! The ekphrastic poem means you'll never be stuck again. Seriously, I am promising the end of writer's block.

"Ekphrasis" is a Greek word meaning image, and "ekphrastic" means "having to do with an image." Ekphrastic poems are just poems that take their starting point from something visual. The first ekphrastic poem is usually thought to be in the *Iliad*, when Achilles is given a shield with a really cool scene engraved on it. The scene kind of comes to life. It's a pretty cool shield. For pages and pages (or papyri and papyri), we are told what the shield looks like and the movement and power of the scene.

Contemporary poets usually write their ekphrastic poems about paintings and art. W. H. Auden wrote a very famous poem that talks about a painting of Icarus, where poor Icarus is just a pair of little white legs disappearing into the ocean. My favorite ekphrastic poem is actually Emma Lazarus's "The New Colossus," about the Statue of Liberty, which is also a sonnet. Emma Lazarus was responding to a poem by Percy Bysshe Shelley about the old Colossus, which is actually a statue of Ozymandias, the Greek name for Egyptian Pharaoh Ramses the second. Obviously, you can combine a lot of different styles and forms of poetry.

Figure 7.1. *The Burghers of Calais*, by Auguste Rodin. This file was donated to Wikimedia Commons as part of a project by the Metropolitan Museum of Art. See the Image and Data Resources Open Access Policy, CC0, https://commons.wikimedia.org/w/index.php?curid=56517

You can find an image anywhere. You can screenshot your phone at random and write about that image. You can pause your television during any show and write about that picture. I love going to an art museum and letting students pick their own paintings to write about. I keep a file of postcards I've purchased while traveling and images that I've cut from magazines, so when I teach the ekphrastic poem to classes that are not in an art museum, I hand out the file and let each student pick out their own image. But since I'm not there, let's use an artwork I love: Auguste Rodin's bronze sculpture *The Burghers of Calais*.

This sculpture was completed by the French artist Auguste Rodin in 1889, to commemorate a historical episode from 1347. After a long siege, the French city of Calais surrendered to the English King Edward III, who demanded that the six leaders of the town sacrifice themselves to save the people of their city. The burghers cared more for their people than for themselves and left the city wearing nooses, ready to be hanged. Edward III's wife demanded mercy for them, and both they and their city suffered no further attacks.

Rodin's sculpture was shocking to his contemporaries, because it was not a heroic or defiant depiction of these men but rather a show of sadness and abject misery. They look like men in the depths of despair, not proud leaders. Of course, this is what I love about the sculpture. Their pain and fear feel so real to me, and so compelling that I cannot look away when I see the piece.

Here are some strategies for approaching an image to write an ekphrastic poem, and I'll use them to approach the Rodin sculpture:

1. Write a monologue in the voice of one of the characters in the image.
2. Tell a story about what's happening in the picture.
3. Describe the image.
4. Imagine how the image was made.

Here are the poems, strategy by strategy.

1. As a monologue:

The Burghers of Calais

In the voice of the Burgher

After eleven months, alas, we need food. After

Eleven months of siege, there is nothing we have

Not tried. After eleven months, we have no choice

And if it means my child can live, then I will not.

If it means my wife can live, then I will not.

If it means my neighbors can live, then I will not.

This rope around my neck is the last thing I will

Feel. This rope around my neck is the weight

Of carrying a city on my back.

2. As a story:

The Burghers of Calais

1347

Do you think it's true? I mean, I have no reason
Not to believe it's true, but these days everyone
Doubts so many things. When I look around me,
I don't see anyone willing to sacrifice themselves
For their people, for their families. It feels like
A story I want to be true, but not for me. I never
Want someone I love to be in that position,
Though I want to believe if it came to that,
They would do that for me, and me for them.

3.   As a description of the image

The Burghers of Calais
   A Description of the Sculpture

There's only one color, the color of bronze,
A dark brown that can be burnished to a bright
Almost gold, a color that speaks of weight
And heft. The men are in a circle, stooped,
Not ashamed, but without pride; not facing
Each other, but not looking in any one direction.
Rodin might have known that in the ancient
World, the marble was brightly painted,
The statues covered with rich hues of blue
And red and gold, but these are men of
Metal, firm in their resolve, frozen in time,
Sacrificing themselves for a sacrifice

That never comes, except in this one moment

The bronze moment they stand in, forever.

4. Imagining how the image was made

The Burghers of Calais

Planning the Sculpture

Rodin asked for the sculpture to placed

On a low pedestal, to be seen framed

By the sky, or on the ground, where

The figures are on the same plane

As the viewer. He wanted the viewer

To feel their pain, to see the abject

Misery, to feel it as their own. What

Does it matter, if one suffers at a height

Or suffers at ground level? It matters

A lot said Rodin. It matters a lot.

I also chose an image by the artist Rodin because he was famously a powerful influence on his secretary, the poet Rainer Maria Rilke. When Rilke was stuck, Rodin told him to go to the zoo and stare at an animal for no less than three hours. The poem that came out of that exercise, "The Panther," was a huge success. Rilke wrote in German, but you can find (and compare) many translations of the poem.

Template

There's really no template for an ekphrastic poem. You could use any other form—sonnets, sestinas, villanelles—if you want to. As long as it's about an image, it's an ekphrastic poem.

A Few Hints for Writing an Ekphrastic Poem

Images are everywhere. A few places you can find an image to write about:

An art museum

An art museum's website

A park or field

A building or house

A train station

The family car (inside or outside)

Basically if you open your eyes and stand in front of it, you can write an ekphrastic poem about it.

When writing an ekphrastic poem, you can use one or all of the techniques laid out in this chapter. My suggestions are summarized:

1. Write a monologue in the voice of one of the characters in the image.
2. Tell a story about what's happening in the picture.
3. Describe the image.
4. Imagine how the image was made.

Exercises

1. Choose a piece of art and have the entire class write about the same artwork.
2. Pause your television and write about the image.

3. Look at the last picture on your phone and write an ekphrastic poem about it.
4. Let your classroom, living room, or bedroom be the image that you write about.
5. Come up with more strategies for how to approach the image and write the poem.

How to Share and Workshop an Ekphrastic Poem

1. You always want to start with the image and talk about how the poem connects to the image.
2. Discuss whether or not you would be able to tell what the image is just from reading the poem.
3. Discuss whether or not knowing the image influences how the reader understands the poem.

8 **Structuring Devices**
Rhythm, Rhyme, and Line

Throughout this book, I've been explaining poetic forms and how those forms also make rhetorical demands. If you have been writing those poems, then you've already been playing with rhythm, rhyme, and lineation. For this section, you will be reconsidering the devices you've already been using, thinking about their history and their use. Most importantly, this section asks you to listen to the way your voice already works.

Rhyme and Other Repeated Sounds

The sounds of any language are arbitrary. There's no reason that the sound "tree" means the word "tree." In Spanish, if you want to make people think of a tree, you say "arbol." In Russian it's "derevo." There's no reason for our words to be the words they are, except that we've all learned them and agreed on them. Rhyme gives order to a system that is arbitrary, similarly to the way the abecedarian gives meaning to the random order in which the letters of the English alphabet are arranged. It's obvious that rhyme helps us remember things, but studies also show that rhymes make people find statements more believable. It's not just that "Haste makes waste" is easy to remember. People are more likely to believe the statement "Haste makes waste" than the statement "Rushing through things means you have to throw out your failed attempts." Rhyme is satisfying because it creates order where there is chaos.

If the last syllable of a word is stressed, then you only need one syllable in order to make a rhyme. The final stressed vowel must be repeated, and if there is a consonant that follows, it must also be repeated.

P**art**/D**art**

Under**neath**/T**eeth**

Sk**y**/Wh**y**

If the second to last syllable is stressed, then you need the last two syllables to repeat in order to have a rhyme.

P*ower*/Fl*ower*

Under/Blunder

G*iggle*/W*iggle*

In a rhyme, we'll always have at least one repeating consonant and one repeating vowel sound, but there are other technical terms for sound repetitions that are useful to know.

Assonance is when vowel sounds repeat.

H*o*ver / S*u*mmer / T*o*n—*the "uh" sound is repeated.*

Consonance is when a consonant sound repeats.

Ho*t*els / Pa*tt*erns / As*tu*te—*the "t" sound is repeated.*

Alliteration is when words all start with the same sound, either a consonant or a vowel.

We **w**ill **w**onder **w**illfully—repeated consonant sounds at the start of the word.

Affective **a**ngers **a**nticipate **a**nswers—repeated vowel sounds at the start of the word.

Sometimes it can be hard to distinguish between a consonant and a vowel. As a general rule, vowels have duration and you can make them long and hold them in your voice. You can say "ooo" or "uh" or "ee" for a while, whereas "k," "g," or "t" are quick sounds that cannot be held. English treats "m," "n," and "s" as consonants even though you can hold them for a long duration.

Rhymes are extremely intuitive, and most of us learn rhymes as children because they are fun and memorable. But remember that rhyme is a special form of repeated sounds at the end of the words, and we can pattern those repetitions in other ways.

Rhythm

Here is the most important thing to keep in mind when writing and reading poems: *rhythm exists in your voice*. Rhythm is a pattern of stressed and unstressed syllables. It is not an external force used exclusively by poets to shoehorn words into demanding structures. Everything that you say, read, or write has a pattern of stresses and unstresses. When we count those rhythms and standardize them, we call that "meter."

In the same way that dancers stylize movement, so that we recognize that the dancer is "walking" or "gardening" or "fighting" from the similarities of our movements in those behaviors, so is meter a stylization of the way we speak.

Also, stress patterns vary by dialect and region. We all know someone who pronounces words differently from us—we usually notice because we find it funny. I have had many people make fun of my Baltimore-inflected, two-syllable pronunciation of the word "school"—I say "skoo-wuhl" stressing both syllables evenly. There are many words in English that offer us variant pronunciations—like "banal" can be "BAY-nal" or "buh-NAHL." "Vase" can be pronounced "VACE" or "VAHZ." There is not a wrong way of speaking, although there is generally a standard range of pronunciation. When looking at the word "luminous," no one says "loo-MIN-us."

We all feel that our way of speaking is "natural," but really, we have to remember that accent and dialect are just differences—they alter our toolset with regard to how we receive and create poetry—but there is no superior or inferior set of word pronunciations. Some rather famous poets—Jean Toomer and Robert Burns come to mind immediately—wrote in dialects that deviate so strongly from standard (or perhaps I should say "standardized") English as to be almost unintelligible to most English speakers. But still, Burns is responsible for our New Year's favorite "Auld lang syng," which is Scottish for "old time's sake." It is important that we remember and respect each other's modes of speech.

Of course, once we start looking at stress, we will mostly be discussing standardized pronunciations, with only minor deviations. Dictionaries mark standard stress for words, and one of my favorite websites, http://yourdictionary.com, will even pronounce words for you if you have a question about standardized pronunciations. And lest we be too distressed over the standardization of English, we should remember that standardization means that we can still read Jane Austen and John Donne in a way we can't still read Chaucer.

Looking at Stress

The first step to understanding meter is understanding stress. For some words, it's easy:

Tiger.

Tiger

This can only be pronounced "TIE-grr." To say "tie-GRRR" would be silly. To find the stress, exaggerate the loudness and softness of each syllable. Even though we don't really say "TIE-ger," we can still hear that the first syllable is louder than the second.

Baseball

Baseball

Again, we can hear the strong difference between the stressed "base" and the unstressed "ball." To say "base-BALL" is not a variant of speech you can expect. It's possible that someone, somewhere is saying "base-BALL," but this is hard enough to get a grip on without making up new dialects. Most words are pronounced with the stress in the same place and do have a stress pattern that we can anticipate.

Go through these words and say them out loud, exaggerating the stress of each until you can figure out where the stress is.

overwhelm

canteen

sorrow

contrive

Obviously, one-syllable words have only one stress, and we'll get to the role they play later.

Terminology

The easiest way to talk about something is to have words for it, so here are the basic terms that we'll use when talking about rhythm.

Feet

A foot is a basic unit of two or three syllables with one or two stresses. We put feet together to get a line. Here are the different kinds of feet:

The Iamb (pronounced "EYE-am")

An iamb is an unstressed syllable followed by a stressed syllable.

> re**view**

> ex**am**

A line which has a general pattern of unstressed syllables followed by stressed syllables is said to be "iambic."

> x / x / x / x / x /
> But **soft** what **light** through **yon**der **win**dow **breaks** ("Romeo & Juliet, Shakespeare 2.2.2")

When the stress is marked about the line, a "/" hovers above each stressed syllable; an "x" or a "U" hovers over unstressed syllables. I wanted to do it so you could see it; however, the formatting of the web is too complicated, so I'll stick to bolding stress when I want to make it visible.

You can see that an iambic line can have words that are not themselves iambic (**yon**der), and that what matters is the pattern across the line. Often when scanning (reading for meter) a poem, people will mark a line between the feet to make it clearer:

*But **soft** | what **light** | through **yon** | der **win** | dow **breaks***

What matters is the pattern formed by the syllables, regardless of the word breaks. The words "but" and "soft" make up one iamb ("but soft"), even though each word is not an iamb on its own. Iambs can split words— "der win"— because we are looking at the syllable pattern of the line independently of the words. I'll only split the feet with vertical lines when I think the feet would be hard to see without them. For the most part, I want you to read the lines smoothly, not stopping between feet.

The trochee (pronounced "trow-key")

A trochee is a stressed syllable followed by an unstressed syllable.

yonder

killer

friendly

A line which has a general pattern of stressed syllables followed by unstressed syllables is said to be "trochaic."

Once up | **on** a | **mid**night | **drear**y ("The Raven," Edgar Allan Poe)

Space to **breathe**, how **short** so**ev**er ("Queen and Huntress," Ben Jonson)

I always get a little chuckle out of the fact that the word "iamb" is a trochee, but it's not exactly a joke you can tell at parties, unless you go to very strange parties.

The Anapest

An anapest is two unstressed syllables followed by a stressed syllable.

over**come**

under**stand**

Anapestic lines follow a general pattern of unstressed, unstressed, stressed.

*Where the **trav** | eller's **jour** | ney is **done*** ("Ah Sun-flower," William Blake)

The Dactyl

A dactyl is a stressed syllable followed by two unstressed syllables.

cauterize

powerful

general

Dactylic lines follow a general pattern of stressed, unstressed, unstressed

Whispering **still** her name ("Eve," by Ralph Hodson)

The Spondee (pronounced "spondee")

A spondee is two stresses together.

out side

come here

A spondee is usually a substitution for another foot.

Naming Lines by Metrical Patterns

We are now in the range of what is called "accentual syllabic" verse. This simply means that we count the number of syllables *and* the number of accents (or stresses).

Now that you know what a foot is, I'll just give you the terms for varying line lengths. Since you are all line length experts by now, I'll not dwell on this part.

Monometer: One Foot per line (very rare)

Dimeter: Two feet per line

Trimeter: Three feet per line

Tetrameter: four feet

Pentameter: five feet

Hexameter: six feet

But Why Doesn't This Always Work?

You may already have found some examples where you would have placed the stress in different places. If you go to your William Shakespeare or Robert Frost, you'll find all kinds of variation or places where you disagree with the "obvious" way to read it. Scansion (reading to find the meter) is not a strict science, and in fact, if a poem's meter is so regular as to become sing-song, the poem will become boring. Let's look at the factors that complicate the perfect metrical world we just laid out.

First, we do have words that don't seem to fit anywhere. Let's look at the word "ice-cream". It can be an iamb, a trochee, or a spondee.

Also, rhythm considers the patterning of louder and softer syllables, but there are many levels of stress in English. It would be easy if there were only two. I often encourage my students to look for strong stresses. Most contemporary poets are more concerned with the rhythms of the poem than with having metrical "correctness."

Understanding the Poetic Line

The idea of a poetic line is actually older than writing! Even though we see lines on the page, the idea of moving back and forth in poetry comes from oral culture, from before writing existed. The word "verse" means "turning," but it refers to the turn of a plow in farming, not the return to the left side of the page when writing. Let's look at a history of the line in English to see the different work that line endings have done over time.

Old English Poetry: 500 AD through 1100 AD

Some people speculate that the earliest Old English poems were rowing songs, designed to keep rowers pulling their paddles in time. In Old English poetry (also called Anglo-Saxon, since "Old English" is a foreign language for speakers of Modern English), the line is composed of two sides, with an alliteration and two strong stresses on either side of a caesura (a pause). Of the four stresses (or beats) in the line, three of the four alliterate. If you like knowing the technical names for things, each half of the line is called a hemistich. Here is a line from "Caedmon's Hymn," which was written sometime between 658 and 680.

> weork Wuldor-Faeder | swa he wundra gehwaes
>
> the work of the Glory-Father, | when he of wonders everyone

You'll have to take my word for it that there are two strong stresses on either side of the caesura, but you can see the alliterations for yourself—all those "h" sounds. Caedmon is the first English poet on record. Though very little "modern" English poetry obeys this strict structure, you can hear the remnants of it in many works. Gerard Manley Hopkins (1844–89) was particularly fascinated by Anglo-Saxon poetics and consciously imitated the alliterative, stressed line. Take, for example, this line:

As kingfishers catch fire, dragonflies draw flame.

Hopkins complicates the basic structure of the Anglo-Saxon line, multiplying the number of beats and consonantal repetitions. You can hear the strong pause in the middle and the "f" sound that moves across the entire line:

As king**f**ishers catch **f**ire, dragon**f**lies draw **f**lame

And, while the left hemistich alliterates the "k" sound—

As **k**ingfishers **c**atch fire, dragonflies draw flame

the right hemistich alliterates the "d" sound—

As kingfishers catch fire, **d**ragonflies **d**raw flame.

More recent experiments in the Anglo-Saxon line have been carried out by such poets as W. H. Auden and Robert Hass. Anglo-Saxon prosody retains a powerful hold on us. Contemporary American poetry has centuries-deep roots, and no poet is ever cut off from the poetic tools that may at first glance appear to have vanished. It's interesting to consider whether a renewed emphasis on stress rather than an emphasis on rhyme or syllabics might help poetry be more accessible to a broader spectrum of English speakers. After all, most words will tend to have the same number of stresses no matter how they're pronounced (i.e., "abDOmen" and "ABdomen" have the same number of stresses).

Middle English Poetry: 1066 to the Late 1400s

In 1066, the Norman Invasion occurred. Despite the rather un-francophone name, the Normans were indeed French and introduced French language (and literature) to the island where our linguistic ancestors were busy speaking Old English and rowing boats. French gradually became the language of the aristocracy and the courts, and alliterative-rhythmic English poetry gained a new device: rhyme. That's right, rhyme was an import, primarily from France.

Chaucer, the most famous and influential of the Middle English poets, was a diplomat and a politician, and was presumably well-versed in the French language. Here are four lines from "The Knight's Tale"—one of the Canterbury Tales told in couplets. These lines describe Theseus's sack of Thebes:

> *And by assuat he wan the citee after*
> And rente adoun bothe wall and sparre and rafter;
> And to the ladyes he restored agayn
> The bones of hir freends that were slayn.

Which I'll translate to:

> *And by assault he won the city after*
> And tore down every wall and beam and rafter
> And to the ladies he restored again
> The bones of their friends that had been slain.

We can also glean from his work that Middle English prosody began to count syllables and to arrange the stressed and unstressed syllables into patterns. Chaucer used a number of different stanza structures, many far more complex than the couplet, but all of them employed an end rhyme. In addition, the exposure to European poetry changed the very subject matter of English poetry, introducing fabliaux and romance. The transition from Old to Middle English saw a dramatic shift in the form and focus of English poetry.

Modern English Poetry: Approximately 1500 through 1900

As you can see from the dates above, Modern English poetry is not the same as Modernism. It began in the Renaissance, and the poetic structures and devices that emerged at the beginning of the period dominated English literature more or less until the advent of the Edwardian/Georgian movements (the bucolic forerunners of Modernism).

It is difficult to draw a clear line between Medieval and Renaissance poetry, in that the change is more gradual and one of growing continental and classical influence. The metric structures that we begin to see in the Medieval period are codified in the Renaissance. One significant arrival is the sonnet, which enters English when Sir Thomas Wyatt translates Petrarch's sonnets in the same poetic structure as Petrarch used. Renaissance poets were particularly interested in the possibility of transposing Greek and Latin poetic structures into English poetry. Milton was so steeped in Latin literature that he sometimes used Latin syntax in his English verse and he eschewed rhyme in his longer works on the principle that the Romans did not use it. William Shakespeare is an exception to this trend. In *The Tempest*, for instance, we can still hear remnants of Anglo-Saxon prosody: "Full fathom five thy father lies." This is from a rhymed poem, with metrical structure, but it retains the strong stress, pause, and alliteration of an earlier era.

Skipping ahead. In the nineteenth century, two Yanks in the poetic court (Emily Dickinson and Walt Whitman) began to break these rules, using irregular rhymes and rhythms. So radical was Whitman's loose poetic line that a fellow poet said Whitman was "as unacquainted with art as a Hog is with mathematics." As funny as his criticism is, it's also telling. The metrical line has a relationship to mathematics. The regularized poetic line is like a verbal equation—with it, a reader can determine if the equation is true (conforming) or false (straying). Whitman violated this rule of recognition, making a poetry that couldn't be evaluated for its mathematical accomplishment.

In some ways, Dickinson looks less radical by comparison. Her poetry does not have the sprawl of Whitman's, but her short lines and off-rhymes have the similar effect of disrupting the metrical expectations of the reader. Dickinson did not publish during her lifetime partially because she would not alter her work to meet the prevailing demands of regularity. In fact, her brother and his wife altered much of Dickinson's work after her death in order to publish it, and there are still debates about just how Dickinson intended her work to appear. It's not entirely surprising that the late 1800s saw a departure from codified understandings of poetry. The second half of the 1800s witnessed the increasing acceptance of Darwin's theories and the stirrings of Marx and Freud. Their ideas collectively challenged the ordering of the world, and many artists felt a need to reorder their work and disrupt their lineation accordingly.

Modernist Poetry and Onward: 1900 through the Present

Modernism is a pretty big concept and, in reality, there were many different modernisms in many different arts. For our purposes, it's useful to focus on the emergence of the free verse line. Again, we have the French to thank. What began as vers libéré (liberated verse) in 1886 with the publication in *La Vogue* of unmetered poems by Rimbaud and Whitman became "vers libre," or "free verse." In other words, you can pretty much break the line anywhere you want to! You may have heard the phrase "Art is what the artists are doing," which means that contemporary art has moved past expected categories like painting and sculpture as artists have embraced eccentric and unusual modes of work. You might also say "Poetry is what the poets are doing," to indicate that in the past hundred and fifty years, you can find almost any kind of writing (including drawings, grids, and lists) calling itself poetry and being accepted as poetry. You have a lot of freedom as a poet, but if you've been doing the exercise, I'm hoping you see the value in traditional poetic forms.

Today most poets use the line break as a way to insert a very small pause, a bit shorter in duration than a comma. The line break can also be used with punctuation to extend a pause. So if a line ends with a period, the pause for the line break is "added" to the pause for the period. For most beginning poets, the most important distinction regarding the line break is between an enjambed line and an end-stopped line. An end-stopped line is when the syntax of the sentence terminates at the end of the line, as in this passage from Walt Whitman's "I Sing the Body Electric":

> Was it doubted that those who corrupt their own bodies conceal themselves?
>
> And if those who defile the living are as bad as they who defile the dead?
>
> And if the body does not do fully as much as the soul?
>
> And if the body were not the soul, what is the soul?

An enjambed line would be when the syntax wraps around the line endings. I hate to violate Whitman's lineation, but for the purpose of illustration, this is what the poem would look like if it *were* enjambed:

> *Was it doubted that those*
> who corrupt their own bodies
> conceal themselves?
> And if those who defile
> the living are as bad as they

> who defile the dead?
> And if the body does not
> do fully as much as the soul?
> And if the body were not
> the soul, what is the soul?

I should be clear that this is *not* what Whitman wrote, but I want to clarify the distinction between end-stopped and enjambed lines. You should definitely take the time to consider what happens when the lineation is changed.

Conclusion

The structuring devices of rhyme, rhythm, and line are very basic to poetry. Poets spend a lot of time considering their impact, and if you continue to work as a poet, you'll find many theories and explanation of these structuring elements. For this introduction, just being aware of them is key, because it allows you to shape them, rather than just doing what feels obvious or natural.

Bibliography

Ali, Agha Shahid. *Call Me Ishmael Tonight: A Book of Ghazals*. New York: Norton, 2003.

Blake, William. "Ah Sun-flower." Poetryfoundation.org

Browning, Elizabeth Barrett. "Sonnet 43." Poets.org

Butson, Denver. "Drowning Ghazals." *Ravishing DisUnities: Real Ghazals in English*. Ed. Agha Shahid Ali, 29–30. Hanover: Wesleyan University Press, 2001.

Chaucer, Geoffrey. "The Knights Tale." Harper Collins, 2013.

Findell, Martin. *Runes*. London: The British Museum, 2014.

"Ghazal: The Charms of a Considered Disunity." *The Practice of Poetry: Writing Exercises from Poets Who Teach*. Ed. Robin Behn and Chase Twichell, 205–9. New York: Harper Collins, 1992.

Hollander, John. *Rhymes Reason*. New Haven and London: Yale University Press, 1981.

Hopkins, Gerard Manley. "As Kingfishers Catch Fire, Dragonflies Draw Flame." Poets.org

Hopkins, Gerard Manley. "Pied Beauty." Poets.org.

Introduction. *Ravishing DisUnities: Real Ghazals in English*. Ed. Agha Shahid Ali, 1–13. Hanover: Wesleyan University Press, 2001.

Jalajel, David. "A Short History of the Ghazal." *The Ghazal Page*, 2007. www.ghazalpage.net/prose/notes/short_history_of_the_ghazal.html

Jonson, Ben. "Queen and Huntress." Poetryfoundation.org.

Lehman, David. *The Last Avante-Garde: the Making of the New York School of Poets*. New York: Doubleday, 1998.

Levin, Phillis, Introduction to *The Penguin Book of the Sonnet*. New York: Penguin Books, 2001.

Peacock, Molly. *How to Read a Poem . . . and Start a Poetry Circle*. New York: Penguin Putnam, 1999.

Poe, Edgar Allen. "An Acrostic." *Poets.org*. (public domain)

Poe, Edgar Allan. "The Raven." Poetryfoundation.org

Ralegh, Sir Walter. "To His Son." *The Penguin Book of the Sonnet*. Ed. Phillis Levin. New York: Penguin Books, 2001.

Schneiderman, Jason. "Filmic Abecedarian with Stutter," *American Poetry Review*, July/August 2008.

Shakespeare, William. *Romeo and Juliet*. Folger.edu

Spanos, Margaret. "The Sestina: An Exploration of the Dynamics of Poetic Structure." *Speculum* 53, no. 3 (July 1978): 545–57.

Whitman, Walt. "I Sing the Body Electric." Poets.org

About the Author

Jason Schneiderman has been teaching poetry for a quarter of a century, working with writers of all ages, from second graders to septuagenarians. He is the author of five books of poems: *Self Portrait of Icarus as a Country on Fire* (2024); *Hold Me Tight* (2020); *Primary Source* (2016), winner of the Benjamin Saltman Prize; *Striking Surface* (2010), winner of the Richard Snyder Prize; and *Sublimation Point* (2004), a Stahlecker Selection. His poetry and essays have appeared in numerous journals and anthologies, including *American Poetry Review*, *The Best American Poetry*, *Poetry London*, and *The Penguin Book of the Sonnet*. He has received fellowships and awards from Yaddo, the Fine Arts Work Center, the Fulbright Foundation, and the Poetry Society of America. He is a co-host of the podcast *Painted Bride Quarterly Slush Pile* and has been a guest host for *The Slowdown*. He is Professor of English at CUNY's BMCC and teaches in the MFA Program for Writers at Warren Wilson College. His book of essays *Nothingism: Poetry at the End of Print Culture* was published by the University of Michigan Press Poets on Poetry imprint in 2025.